LANCASTER
in action

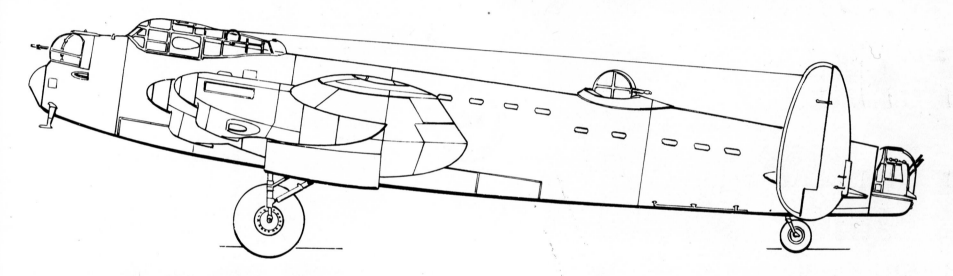

by R.S.G. Mackay
illustrated by Don Greer

 squadron/signal publications

EA⊙U flown by Flight Lieutenant W. Hay of 49 Sqdn., equipped with A.G.L.T. rear turret code named 'Village Inn', and based at Fulbeck (Lincolnshire), Nov. 1944.

ROYAL AIR FORCE
BOMBER COMMAND

ISBN 0-89747-130-X

If you have any photographs of the aircraft, armor, soldiers or ships of any nation, particularly wartime snapshots, why not share them with us and help make Squadron/Signal's books all the more interesting and complete in the future. Any photograph sent to us will be copied and the original returned. The donor will be fully credited for any photos used. Please send them to: Squadron/Signal Publications, Inc., 1115 Crowley Dr., Carrollton, TX 75006.

Photo Credits:

I.W.M.	M. Middlebrook
J.C. Scutts	D. Brett
B. Robertson	Helmut Rosenboom
British Official	G. Stafford
J. MacKintosh	G. Copeman
C. Clarke	C. Bishop
D. Clarke	H. Holmes
J. Edwards	A. Simpson
I. McTaggart	L. Young
G. Henry	A.T. Douglas
A. Howell	K. Batchelor
M.L. Gibson	G. Cunningham
C. Hall	RAF Museum
Canadian Forces	G. Russell
C. Koder	J. Flynn
	L. Moore

VN⊙N/F5689 of 50 Squadron displays to the Press in mid-1942 on the occasion of the Lancaster's public debut. Note the early style pitot mast and the wing walkway lines. This bomber was written off on 19 September 1942 when she crashlanded on approach at Swinderby. (I.W.M.)

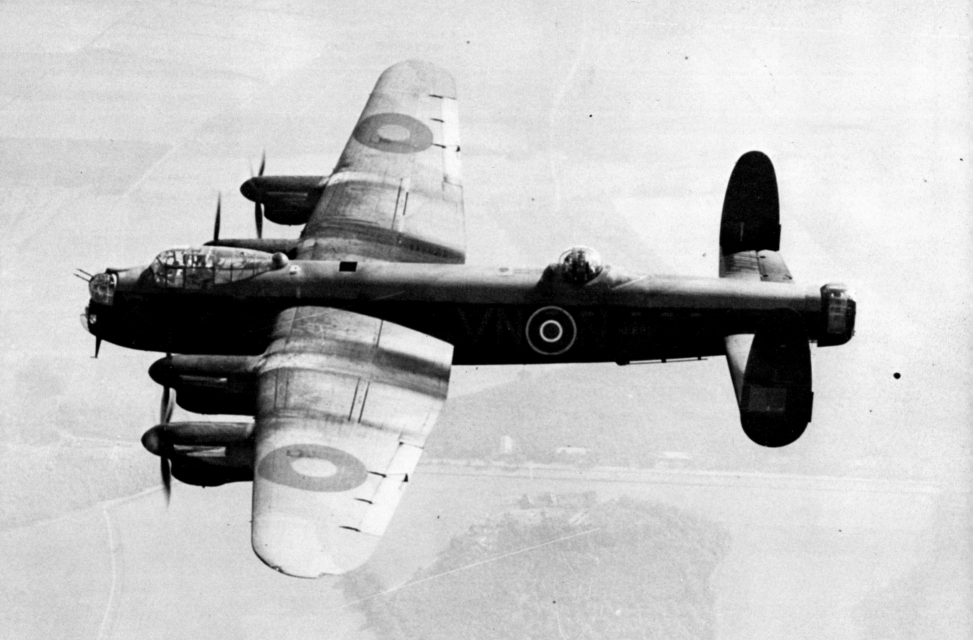

Introduction

The Lancaster bomber holds a special place of affection mingled with a great deal of pride in the hearts of British and Commonwealth citizens — feelings which perhaps find their parallel in the hearts of Americans toward the B-17 Flying Fortress. Just as the Spitfire epitomized the Commonwealth's supreme spirit of defiance in the face of seemingly irresistible defeat, so the evening sight and sound of streams of Lancasters "heading out" toward the heartland of the German Reich was the ultimate translation of a war-weary people's will to see the Nazi military and industrial machine — the source of colossal suffering for so much of the world — battered into oblivion.

Like all successful aircraft the Lancaster not only looked good but its flying characteristics matched its appearance. It is all the more ironic therefore that the birth of Avro's mighty machine owed so much to failure, the failure of its immediate predecessor, the **Manchester**.

In May 1936 Group Captain R.D. Oxland, Director of the Air Ministry's Operational Requirements, issued specification P.13/36 for a twin engine bomber capable of carrying internally a 12,000LB maximum bomb load, or a single 8,000LB bomb, or a pair of torpedoes. Two firms were invited to build prototypes of their design submissions, Handley Page their HP 56 and the Avro 679, in the event the HP 56 was rejected because of a projected shortage of Rolls-Royce engines. Within weeks of Avro receiving a prototype order a production order was placed for 200 machines to the new Specification 19/37.

Large when compared with other twin engine aircraft the P.13/36 was actually powered by four Rolls-Royce engines. Under the designation Vulture, Rolls-Royce had mated a pair of V 12 cylinder Kestrel engines with a common crankcase creating a 24 cylinder V engine and a lot of trouble. On 25 July 1939 the prototype, L7246, was flown for the first time with Group Captain H.A. Brown at the controls. While only airborne for 17 minutes it was long enough to realize that the Vulture engines were turning out much less power than anticipated and wing loading made the aircraft extremely difficult to fly.

To correct lateral instability a central fin was added to the second prototype, L7247, which flew for the first time on 26 May 1940. The second machine was armed with six .303 Browning machine guns, two in the nose, ventral and tail turrets. Production quickly followed with the first production machine, L7276, rolling out on 5 August 1940 during the height of the Battle of Britain. Production machines had a wing span increase and the ventral turret was removed to the dorsal position. The need for additional modifications and the urgency of manufacturing fighters slowed down production of the P.13/36, which was now known as the Manchester. L7277, the second production machine, was not delivered until 25 October 1940.

This second production machine was delivered to No. 207 Squadron at Waddington under the command of Wing Commander Hyde, which had been reformed to work up the still secret Manchester. By the end of the year No. 207 Squadron had received some twenty machines. On 9 January 1941 the existence of the Manchester was revealed to the full RAF and on 24 February six Manchesters were part of the attacking force raiding Brest where a Hipper class cruiser was reported. All machines returned safely but L7284 crash landed at Waddington when the hydraulic system failed. Trouble with the hydraulic system persisted, but was eventually traced to an oil leak which fouled the undercarriage microswitches and was corrected.

An Avro Manchester of 207 Squadron showing the three-fin configuration carried over to the prototype Lancaster, and the cockpit radio mast borne by the prototype and first production Lancaster. Note shape of the Vulture engines, primary cause of the Manchester's demise and emergence of the Lancaster. (J.C. Scutts)

Problems with the Vulture powerplants were not so easily solved however, and No. 207 Squadron seldom had more than five machines serviceable at one time. On the night of 13 March 1941 the first Manchester was lost to enemy action when L7319 was shot down shortly after take-off from Waddington by Feldw. Hans Hahn of I/NJG 2.

Most of the Manchester's mechanical problems by now had been solved and a second assembly line, at Metropolitan Vickers, began turning out machines and new Squadrons were being assembled. The basic problem with the Manchester, that of being underpowered, was still to be addressed. With a service ceiling of only 10,000 feet the loss of one engine resulted in an almost immediate loss of height. This poor performance of the Manchester caused one squadron to (only half-jokingly) plan their squadron reunion in POW camp.

In April all Manchesters were grounded when faults were found in the Vulture engine bearings. On 16 June the Manchesters were again grounded to modify the cooling system and again on 30 June for complete engine overhauls and testing, the results of which were a further series of modifications.

On 7 August operations were resumed at which time two further faults showed up. The tail flutter, which was eventually corrected by redesigning the tail to an enlarged twin fin configuration under the designation **Manchester IA**, and the propeller feathering problem which was not so easily traced. Engine problems seemed to increase rather than abate and casualties grew.

During initial trials of the Manchester prototype it had been quickly realized that the 24 cylinder Vultures were not turning out the anticipated power. Two projects were initiated to correct the situation, replacement of the Vultures with a pair of Napier Sabre or Bristol Centaurus engines keeping the twin engine configuration under the designation Manchester Mk II, or by reconfiguring the aircraft to a four engine machine under the designation Manchester Mk III. The four engine solution was completed first and so successfully that the twin engine projects were dropped out of hand.

BT308, a standard Manchester airframe, was fitted with a new wing center section into which were installed four of the very reliable Rolls-Royce Merlin X engines. Flying for the first time on 9 January 1941, that flight was enough to convince Roy Dobson and his designers that true success had been achieved.

The doubling from two to four motors meant an increase in the Manchester's maximum bomb load, from 10,350LBS to an operational average of 12,000/14,000LBS. Fuel capacity was increased from 1700 to 2154 gallons and range increased from 1200 miles to 2350 miles. Bomber Command now had a bomber that could penetrate deep into Nazi occupied Europe with a much larger bomb load and reasonably expect to evade or fight off all that the enemy could provide in defensive measures — and at an altitude more than double the Manchester's meager 10,000 foot ceiling. Of even more importance to the crews flying the bomber into enemy air space was the security afforded them by the reliability of the newly installed Merlin power plants.

Official testing at Boscombe Down during March found that the elevators and ailerons responded well at either end of an I.A.S. range of 100 to 290MPH, but rudder pressure did increase with speed. The strong tendency to swing to port during take-off was solved by advancing the port-outer throttle and raising the tail quickly, to allow the pilot to bring the rudders into play.

In May the second prototype, DG595, took to the air. In contrast to BT308, she carried both mid-upper and ventral turrets and a newly designed and enlarged twin tail configuration which discarded the center fin. New 1,280HP Merlin XX engines had been installed in place of the earlier Merlin Xs. The RAF now had a bomber with which it could wage war *in Germany*. There would be no more talk around the squadrons about reunions in POW camp!

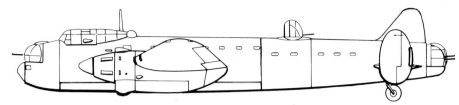

Manchester Mk I

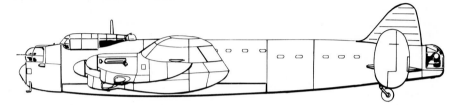

Lancaster Prototype BT308

DG595 shows off her effective camouflage pattern which extends to the fins but excludes the port wing tip. Camouflage pattern was not adopted on production aircraft. Fuselage roundels are oversize. (B. Robertson)

Lancaster Development

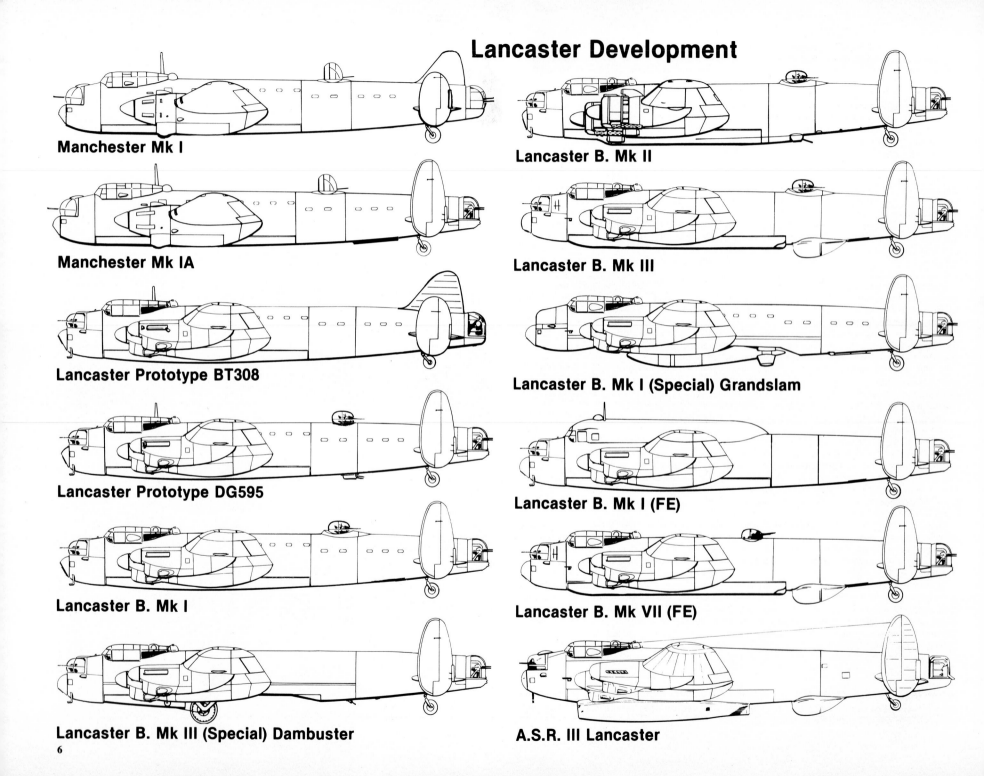

Manchester Mk I

Lancaster B. Mk II

Manchester Mk IA

Lancaster B. Mk III

Lancaster Prototype BT308

Lancaster B. Mk I (Special) Grandslam

Lancaster Prototype DG595

Lancaster B. Mk I (FE)

Lancaster B. Mk I

Lancaster B. Mk VII (FE)

Lancaster B. Mk III (Special) Dambuster

A.S.R. III Lancaster

Lancaster Mk I

On the basis of the prototype's initial performance the new four-engined machine was renamed Lancaster and, using unfinished Manchester airframes, ordered into immediate full scale production upon the completion of the 200th Manchester. The order was more easily placed by Air Ministry than filled by A.V. Roe however. Most of the spring and summer was spent organizing a Lancaster manufacturing group consisting of A.V. Roe, Metropolitan-Vickers, Austin Motors, Vickers-Armstrong and Armstrong-Whitworth together with some 600 subcontractors. L7527, the first *production* Lancaster lifted off at Avro's Woodford airfield on 31 October 1941. Unlike the prototype which had been powered by a quartet of 1,130HP Merlin X engines, production machines were powered by four 1,280HP Merlin XX engines. Air screws were three-bladed De Havilland D.H. 5/40 variable pitch but were interchangeable with the Hamilton A 5/138 propellers. Defensive armament consisted of nine Browning .303 machine guns mounted in four Frazer-Nash hydraulically operated turrets: a pair of .303s in a nose mounted FN5 turret, a pair of .303s in a FN50 mid-upper turret, a single .303 in a FN64 ventral turret and four .303s in a FN20 tail turret. Offensively the Lancaster inherited a cavernous 33 foot single cell bomb bay from the Manchester capable of accepting eight 1,000LB bombs. An armored bulkhead was fitted across the center section of the fuselage, the pilot seat and turret were armor protected as were numerous critical areas within the fuselage.

The second prototype, DG595, was a *true* Lancaster and as such was sent to Boscombe Down for extensive testing, while the first prototype, BT308, the converted Manchester, on 9 September was sent to No. 44 (Rhodesia) Squadron at Waddington to provide air and ground crew an exciting introduction to the new four-engine bomber. No. 44 Squadron of No. 5 Group had been selected to convert from the Hampden to the new heavy and while another three months would elapse before the first three Lancasters, L5737, L5738 and L5741 would arrive, the Squadron was electric with excitement. A combination of thorough training and bad weather delayed the *Lanc's* operational debut until 3 March 1942, when four aircraft, L7546, L7547, L7566 and L7549 of No. 44 Squadron, were sent to lay mines off Heligoland. All returned safely. The first land target was attacked on the night of 10/11 March when two machines from 44 Squadron were among the raiders dispatched to Essen. This mission marked the first of over 156,000 sorties carried out by Lancasters against the Axis during the next three years.

Following the Air Ministry plan of re-equipping 5 Group totally with the new bomber, No. 97 Squadron at Coningsby was next in line for conversion and began trading in their Manchesters in January 1941, becoming operational on the Lancaster in late March.

The public was still unaware that Bomber Command had a new heavy bomber and Air Ministry took the occasion of a successful if costly daylight mission to unveil their new weapon to both the Third Reich and the British public. Just before 3PM on 17 April six machines each from 44 and 97 Squadrons were dispatched to carry out a daring daylight raid against the submarine engine producing M.A.N. plant at Augsburg, deep inside Germany. In four formations of three each the bombers "headed out" toward Bavaria. There and back would mean some 1500 miles of flying, *over enemy* territory. Just after crossing the channel No. 44 Squadron was attacked by fighters. L7536 in the first V was the first to go down, then one after another No. 44's second V, R5506, L7548 and L7565, was shot

The prototype Lancaster, her original three fins now replaced by the standard twin fin layout, displays in front of Winston Churchill at Northolt in July 1941. Tail turret is a FN4A fitting common to Manchesters and was superceded on Lancasters by the FN20. Note absence of pitot mast from lower port nose (normal location on early Mk I bombers). (I.W.M.)

Close-up of the first production Lancaster, L5727, reveals unshrouded exhausts and absence of mesh covers to the carburetor air intakes, such covers acting as ice guards. Aircraft bears similar camouflage pattern to both prototype Lancasters. (British Official)

Flying all night 6, 8, sometimes 12 hours, deep into enemy territory through flak, bad weather, and often having to take violent evasive action to avoid lurking night fighters, severely taxed the ground crews who worked long hours to keep their charges airworthy. (I.W.M.)

Rain and dirt streaks on the original all-enclosed turrets badly, and in some cases fatally, compromised the gunner's visibility. Initial solution seen on this turret was the addition of a sliding panel. Later the entire perspex was removed on many turrets, the resultant enhanced visibility being well worth the marginal temperature drop borne by the already frozen gunner. (British Official)

(Top Right) An early example of a Lancaster, EA ⊙ D serialed ED441 of 49 Squadron shows up the distinctively light exhaust streaking. On the wing leading edges is a liberal but neat application of de-icing paste, later aircraft had thermal de-icing equipment. (British Official)

Frazier-Nash Turrets

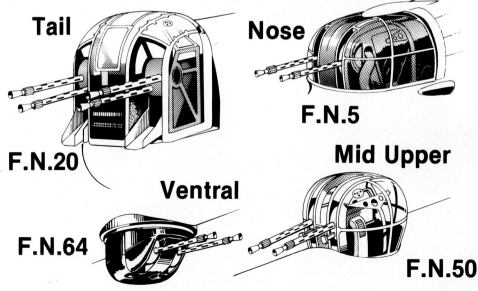

Tail

F.N.20

Nose

F.N.5

Ventral

F.N.64

Mid Upper

F.N.50

down. Determined, but with little hope of reaching their target, the two remaining aircraft closed up and pressed on. Once away from the coastal area, however, the remaining two machines had few problems until the sirens at Augsburg announced their arrival. Going in at chimney top level the two raiders were literally unable to miss. Meeting heavy defensive fire R5510 was set on fire and went down about two miles outside of town.

Having taken a different route to the target, 97 Squadron had avoided the coastal based fighters, and swept in at 400 feet just as No. 44 Squadron Leader Nettleton dropped his bombs. No. 97 Squadron Leader Sherwood, in L7573 was hit over the target and crashed North of Augsburg. R5513 was set on fire while still a mile from the target and was engulfed in flames just after bombing the factory. Heading toward France and into the gloom of dusk, the return journey was under a cloak of darkness.

Four *Lancs* from No. 97 Squadron and one from No. 44 Squadron returned. Squadron Leader Nettleton received the Victoria Cross for leading his Squadron. But, in the words of Sir Arthur Harris "...any operation which deserves the V.C. is in the nature of things unfit to be repeated at frequent intervals..." and while "...Seven out of twelve Lancasters were missing, a loss which was not excessive in proportion to the importance of the objective and the serious damage that was done to it, but [it] did demonstrate beyond all question that daylight attacks on Germany could at that time only be carried out by Bomber Command at a prohibitive casualty rate." The BBC carried news of the attack and of the new bomber while the Germans were sifting through the wreckages of the RAF's new four engine bomber.

As with all new aircraft the Lancaster met problems. A diving test that led to the crash of R5539 was traced to tail-plane surface failure. Fracturing wing tips had to be strengthened and fuel pump blockages affected its ability to reach operational height. Without the aid of service manuals slackness in servicing led to several take-off accidents. However the basic durability of the *Lanc's* design enabled it to ward off these troubles without affecting operational availability at Squadron level. In the words of William Green "Development of the Lancaster airframe from its original Mk I form was dictated almost solely by operational requirements, and it speaks volumes for the basic soundness of the bombers design that few modifications were required for technical reasons, and little could be done to further improve the aircraft's aerodynamics."

Early bombers entering service were notable for their cleanliness of line. Allowing for cockpit and turret protrusions, the only excrescences were the pitot mast, dipole aerial mounted under the rear fuselage and the trailing aerial sheath behind the starboard wing. These early machines had a maximum speed of 275MPH fully loaded at 15,000FT providing a general performance well ahead of either the Stirling or the current Halifax series. The Short Stirling would eventually be phased out of service in favor of the *Lanc* but late Halifax variants would equal the Lancaster in everything but bomb capacity.

The mid-upper turret was at first unfaired; the resultant danger arising from unlimited depression of the guns led, in late 1942, to the fitting of a contoured fairing incorporating a tracking guide to insure that the guns could not train on any part of the bomber. The FN64 ventral turret, because of poor visibility and lack of a regular crew member to constantly man the position, led to its being removed during the course of 1942. The rows of rectangular windows, a carry over from the Manchester, were retained; often being painted over, although the forward pair of windows were deleted from the JB/LM production series onward.

Throughout 1942 the re-equipment of 5.Group was largely affected. A small number of Lancasters bore an enlarged bomb aimers blister with a shallower angled optically flat bomb aimers panel. To accommodate the first 8,000LB bombs, specially designed bulged bomb bay doors began to appear on selected aircraft, and although the first operational dropping of an 8,000 pounder was done by a Halifax the capacious 33 foot single-cell bomb bay of the Lancaster offered nearly limitless possibilities in carrying the various types of ordnance available to the RAF during the war.

Bearing an unfaired mid-upper, OL⊙E serialed R5669 of 83 Squadron lines up for take-off on Scampton's grassy surface during the summer of 1942. No. 83 had received Manchesters in early 1942 but within months these were replaced with Lancasters. In August of 1942 this Squadron moved to Wyton becoming one of the four founder units of No. 8 (Pathfinder) Group. (I.W.M.)

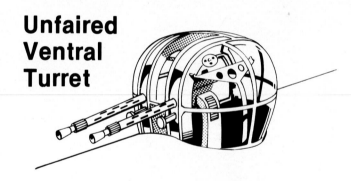

Unfaired Ventral Turret

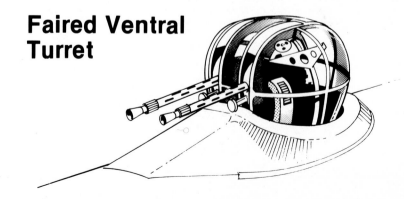

Faired Ventral Turret

Two armourers of No. 106 Squadron prepare a 1,000LB bomb for hoisting into the cavernous 33FT bomb bay of a Lancaster. Armourer on the right is preparing the rear bomb release connection which plugged into the aircraft's electrical system when the bomb was in place. (British Official)

No. 106 Squadron was based at Syerston under the command of Guy Gibson. These two ground crewmen are recharging LN⊙D's oxygen system. (British Official)

TAIL DEVELOPMENT

Manchester

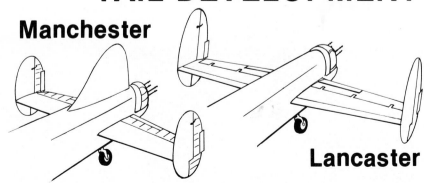

Lancaster

Small bomb containers carrying incendiaries are pulled out to be loaded aboard Lancasters of 460 Squadron. (British Official)

11

A port-outer Merlin hangs over the purposeful outline of three sister Lancasters of 57 Squadron at East Kirkby, fully loaded and awaiting their crews as the evening shadows lengthen. (British Official)

97 Squadron's OF⊙P serialed R5552 carries a witch riding a bomb and forty-seven mission markers. The original RDM2 paint applied to early aircraft such as R5552 was prone to peeling.

A No. 106 Squadron aircraft, believed to be M Mother taxis back to dispersal on its inboard engines on return from Berlin during January 1943. The absence of the mid-upper turret fairing indicates a long serving early production aircraft. (D. Clarke)

R5700 of 106 Squadron coded ZN⊙G is seen undergoing repairs after bellying in at Hardwick upon return from the 13/14 January 1943 raid on Essen. The square compartment on the starboard wing is the dinghy stowage. The IFF wires running to points just below the turret fairing can be seen. R5700 went missing on 22 September of 1943. (British Official)

Lucky to be home after tangling with a night fighter during the 4 December 1943 raid on Leipzig, the crew of VN⊙O pose in front of their damaged machine. ED470 has her tail jacked up and a spare tire wheel can be seen behind and to the left of the crew. (British Official)

Belonging to 49 Squadron, ED805 has run off the narrow 50 foot Fiskerton perimeter track. Recovery was effected by a fuel bowser only to have her go missing during the 16/17 August 1943 raid on Peenemunde. Bomber Command lost 41 aircraft this night but heavily damaged the German rocket research center. (J. Edwards)

(Above and Below) This severely damaged Lancaster was put down at Hardwick by P/O Britton on 21 October 1943, a tribute to the Lancaster's ability to absorb punishment and still come home. (I. McTaggart)

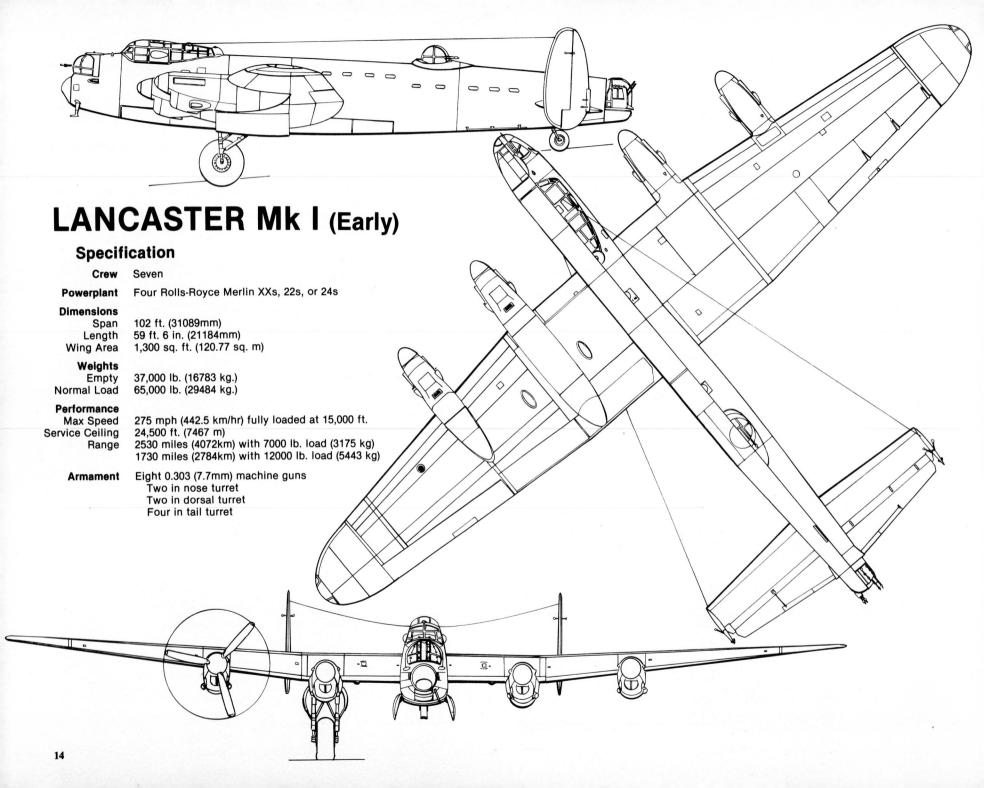

LANCASTER Mk I (Early)

Specification

Crew	Seven
Powerplant	Four Rolls-Royce Merlin XXs, 22s, or 24s

Dimensions
Span   102 ft. (31089mm)
Length   59 ft. 6 in. (21184mm)
Wing Area 1,300 sq. ft. (120.77 sq. m)

Weights
Empty   37,000 lb. (16783 kg.)
Normal Load 65,000 lb. (29484 kg.)

Performance
Max Speed   275 mph (442.5 km/hr) fully loaded at 15,000 ft.
Service Ceiling 24,500 ft. (7467 m)
Range   2530 miles (4072km) with 7000 lb. load (3175 kg)
           1730 miles (2784km) with 12000 lb. load (5443 kg)

Armament   Eight 0.303 (7.7mm) machine guns
          Two in nose turret
          Two in dorsal turret
          Four in tail turret

Mk II

With the advent of full scale Lancaster production, the extra demand placed on Rolls-Royce Merlin supplies raised the spectre of an ultimate bottleneck occurring. That this bottleneck never occurred owes much to the Bristol company and its Hercules radial engine. Four of these Bristol Radials were fitted to BT810 and flight tested on 26 November 1941 with good general results. Since Avro production lines were fully committed to Mk Is, a contract bid from Armstrong-Whitworth was accepted. Between September 1942 and March 1944, A.W. built 300 aircraft at Baginton, serialed DS601-852 and LL617-739.

Apart from DS601-627, which were powered by Hercules VIs, the standard engine was the Hercules XVI. Both powerplants were 14 cylinder sleeve-valve units rated at 1735HP swinging Rotal airscrews which in contrast to the Merlin airscrews, rotated counter-clockwise.

The outline of the Mk II was initially similar to the Mk I/III, but in the early production stage bulged bomb-doors were introduced as standard on the Mk II to accommodate 8,000LB bombs. H2S sets were not carried; instead, the first trials of G-H (a navagational/blind bombing refinement of GEE which gave precise accuracy in functions) were conducted on Mk IIs. (G-H was only trial-tested on Mk II operations, however, with full scale introduction to 3.Group coming only in late 1944.) The absence of H2S allowed the re-introduction of FN64 belly turrets, arguably the most important gun position during 1943/44 operations when schrage Musik came into wide spread use against Bomber Command. FN20 rear turrets were generally replaced by FN120 units of lighter construction and improved gun-sighting mechanisms. Other refinements involved the engines; bell-shaped spinner covers were fitted and Beaufighter patterned air intakes and flame-damping exhausts were introduced. Photographic evidence indicates that the Mk IIs carried the shallow nose blister and early pattern pitot mast.

At an all up weight of 63,000LBS the performance of the Mk II was akin to that of the Mk I/III, realizing a maximum speed of 265MPH at 14,000FT and cruising at 167MPH. The Mk II had a superior rate of climb up to 18,000FT, but progress above this level fell off quickly — an unhealthy position over the target with Merlin powered Mk Is and IIIs operating at upwards of 20,000FT! On the positive side the air-cooled Hercules could sustain a greater degree of damage than its oil-cooled Merlin partner and the barbed exhausts cut down exhaust glow.

Initial operations with the new radial engined Lanc were carried out by a flight from No. 61 Squadron, the first sortie being conducted by DS607 on 11 January 1943 which aborted. The Mk II was officially operational when on the night of 16 January two of the three machines dispatched bombed their German target. The first fully equipped Mk II Squadron was No. 115 which began equipping in March of 1943. Over the next six months Nos. 408, 426 and 432 Squadrons, all from No. 6 (Canadian) Group, followed suit. All four units had previously flown radial-engined Wellingtons or Hampdens, which meant a minimum of ground crew re-training. The final Mk II Squadron was No. 514 formed in September 1943.

In November 1943 Armstrong-Whitworth discontinued Mk II production and converted to Merlin-powered Mk I/III production, a move in part made by the priority demand for the Hercules engine to power the Halifax Mk III. The three Canadian Mk II Squadrons were subsequently converted to the new Halifax variant between February and August of 1944, while Nos. 115 and 514 converted to Merlin-powered Lancs in May and September respectively. During its relatively short operational career the Mk II played a full part in the crucial Battles of the Ruhr, Hamburg, Berlin, the pre-invasion Transportation Plan and the ground support raids following D-Day. Of the 300 Mk II bombers built, no less than 60% were lost on operations. Relegation to Heavy Conversion Units was the general fate of surviving Lancaster IIs, but ten were used as instructional airframes and several served as experimental units. The Mk II was finally declared obsolete in May 1945, but, even then a handful soldiered on as engine and equipment test beds. By 1950 only LL735 was left and she was scrapped that year.

DS652 of 115 Squadron runs up her engines in dispersal at East Wretham. The early style air intakes seen on this machine were soon replaced by the lighter and more efficient Beaufighter pattern intakes. (I.W.M.)

ENGINE DEVELOPMENT

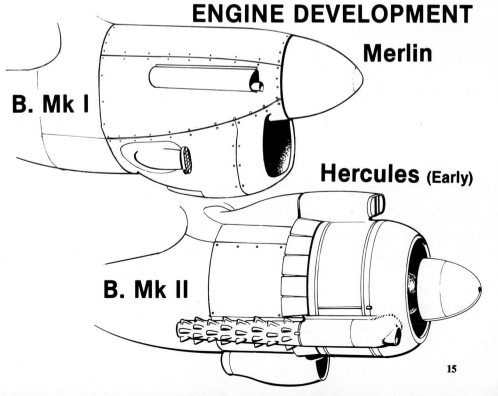

Merlin

B. Mk I

Hercules (Early)

B. Mk II

Very early in the Mk II production run the Beaufighter pattern air intake became standard. (British Official)

Demonstrating the power of the Hercules, DS704 is sustained aloft solely by her No. 1 engine. This machine was allotted to No. 408 (Goose) Squadron and was posted missing on 20/21 December 1943. (G. Henry)

Mk II ENGINES

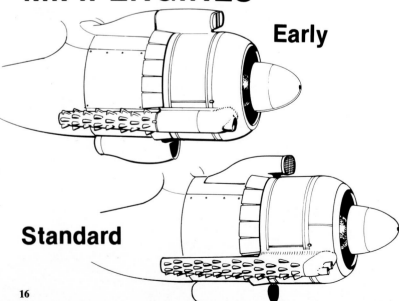

Early

Standard

KO⊙A of No. 115 Squadron with the C.O., Wing Commander Sims at the controls. Walkway lines on the wings extended out into the roundels. Serialed DS685 this machine was one of the thirty aircraft shot down during the final raid against Hamburg on the night of 2/3 August. (A. Howell)

A line-up of 514 Squadron at Waterbeach prior to a Berlin raid in January 1944. The distinctive shape of the B. Mk IIs bulged bomb bay can be seen on the nearest Lancaster. The barbed exhaust was more effective in dissipating heat and consequently glowed less in the night sky. (G. Henry)

BOMBAY

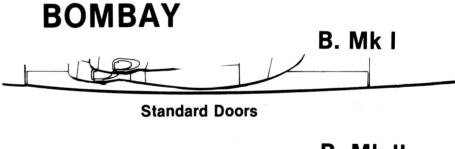

B. Mk I

Standard Doors

B. Mk II

Bulged Doors

(Above Left) About to touch down at Sudbury, the home of the U.S. 486th Bomb Group is *Fanny Ferkin II* of No. 514 Squadron. Coded JI⊙F/DS842, she was written off during March 1945. (I. McTaggart)

Fanny Ferkin II, its cavernous 33 foot bomb bay receiving a covetous inspection by ordnance men of the U.S. 401st Bomb Group at Deenethorpe. (M.L. Gibson)

This machine of 115 Squadron was brought home by Sgt. Jolly, minus its rear turret and its unfortunate occupant. The protrusion of the rear fairing on the bulged bomb bay doors of the Mk II can be seen well. (British Official)

Believed to be JI⊙J serialed LL669 of 514 Squadron is a sorry sight after crash landing at Leiston. Brought in by Sgt. Medland on 17 March 1944, the undercarriage has been shorn off and the wooden Jablo propeller blades have been shattered. (I.W.M.)

Bomber Command operated three emergency airfields on the east coast of England. Probably at Woodbridge, an assortment of Lancasters, Halifaxes and Stirlings can be seen below this Lancaster wing under repair. (British Official)

At the same emergency facility, a B. Mk I undergoes repair work while a Mk II sits patiently in the background. The Mk I's outer starboard engine has been removed for replacement while the inner undergoes major work. (British Official)

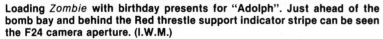

Loading *Zombie* with birthday presents for "Adolph". Just ahead of the bomb bay and behind the Red threstle support indicator stripe can be seen the F24 camera aperture. (I.W.M.)

(Above Right) Calling at Rougham, home of the U.S. 94th Bomb Group, 426 Squadron's OW⊙S does not seem to have made an emergency landing. Serialed DS689 she was missing after the 7 October 1943 raid on Stuttgart. (C. Hall)

As the sun sets in the background, crewmen of No. 426 Thunderbirds head for their aircraft and another mission into Germany. (Canadian Forces Photo)

Lancaster B. Mk III

During the first twelve months of operational service Lancaster production and replacement relied solely on Rolls Royce for supplies of Merlin engines. Supply shortage possibilities, plus the fact that the 18,000 engines per year rate was insufficient, led to an agreement with the US for Packard to produce the Merlin engine under license. Discussions between Rolls and the Ford Motor Company had taken place even before the Lancaster had been evolved and blue prints had been in the States since the fall of France. While British sources have claimed that the Americans at first had difficulty working to Rolls-Royce tolerances, Packard amazed Rolls Royce by producing the first engine within 12 months.

Under the RAF designation Merlin 28 and the USAAF designation Packard V-1650-1, Packard built a two speed supercharged engine capable of delivering 1,420HP at take-off. The original plan was that the engines should be interchangeable but because the parts could not be produced in time, the Packard built Merlins were equipped with an American magneto and a Bendix carburetor.

Lancaster production was such that both US and British produced engines were used as quickly as they became available. When American Packard produced engines were installed the Lancaster was designated a Mk III. There were no external differences and when the engine cowls were in place only a checking of the serial number against manufacturer's lists of what they produced could show the difference; Mk Is and Mk IIIs were run on the same assembly lines at the same time. A Mk I became a Mk III by a simple change of its engines, or vice versa and occasionally even an aircraft with two Merlin and two Packard engines would come out of a repair facility.

Initial air tests using the Packard-produced engines were made in late 1942 by R5849 and W4114 with production installation beginning in mid-1943 with the roll out of W4983. While the US and British Merlins were interchangeable there were varying operational characteristics which somewhat limited their interchangeability at the squadron level. The Packard motor had a more positive starting capacity due to the Stromberg pressure-injection carburetor, but tended to overheat during regular take off and landing, hence the Rolls-Royce powered Mk Is dominant presence among Heavy Conversion Units and Lancaster Finishing Schools which put their aircraft through repeated take off and landing exercises. Mk IIIs began to enter squadron service in December 1943.

Lancaster B. Mk I/Mk III

The introduction of H2S during 1943 — initially to Pathfinder Force aircraft then to Main Force — caused the first regular and prominent change in outline to the Lancaster. Since the set scanners extended below the rear fuselage, a half pear-shaped fairing was fitted. Made of perspex, the rear section was unpainted to allow the enclosed identification lights to be seen. H2S was a downward looking radar set based on a high power magnetron valve that received echoes more strongly from built-up areas than from flat countryside. The echoes received by the rotating aerial system were displayed on a cathode-ray tube that traced a representation of the countryside below, very nearly a map that could be traced on the cathode ray tube right through cloud cover.

The 1943 Battles of the Ruhr and Hamburg realized heavy destruction of German industrial resources but only at a steadily rising loss ratio caused primarily by Luftwaffe Night Fighters. To supplement the rear gunner's visual search an arrow-shaped aerial was fitted below the rear turret. Under the code name *Monica*, this new device was a rearward looking radar set designed to provide warning of fighter aircraft in a 45 degree angle. However, the device's inability to differentiate between friendly and hostile aircraft and the discovery that the Germans could home on the apparatus led to its withdrawal.

Window

During the battle of Hamburg an initially very effective means of blinding Luftwaffe radar, both ground and airborne, completely paralyzed German night defenses. *Window* was used to put out the eyes of the defenders and H2S was used to find the target. Hamburg was subjected to four main attacks, 3,095 sorties, dropping some 9,000 tons of bombs on the city—killing over fifty thousand people, destroying half the buildings, and leaving almost a million people homeless. British losses were 87 aircraft, 2.8%, which was much lower than the usual 6% losses experienced by Bomber Command when attacking Hamburg.

CF⊙X of 625 Squadron serialed LM 384 was one of the last aircraft to arrive on station without being factory fitted with H2S. Seen in December 1943, she was Missing In Action over Leipzig on 19/20 February 1944, the Luftwaffe had put nearly 300 night fighters into the air and 78 bombers failed to return. (C. Koder)

Fitted with H2S on the rear under belly and seen at Fiskerton in Mid-1944, ND787 of 49 Squadron displays her codes in the standard starboard position. (T. Edwards)

H2S

Window was aluminum foil stiffened with a black paper backing and cut into strips 30 centimeters long by 1.5 centimeters wide. The silvery side was coated with lampblack so the clouds of aluminum foil would not show up in the searchlight beams but would still reflect radar waves. Initially window was dispatched through any convenient aperture in the aircraft, however within weeks Lancs were fitted with a louvered box structure on the lower starboard side of the nose through which the Window was distributed by either the Flight Engineer or the Bomb Aimer.

By late 1943 Bomber Command was committed to regular deep penetration raids, the majority of sorties being flown by Lancasters, deemed to be the only heavy capable of striking targets while bearing acceptable loss-ratios. The early war decision to fit British bombers with .303 machine guns now meant that Lancasters were at a serious disadvantage when locked in combat with cannon armed night fighters. Unknown to Bomber Command the Luftwaffe's Night Fighter arm had developed devices to home on both H2S and Monica, and developed *schrage Musik,* an upward firing armament. This new German device took a terrible toll of Lancasters during the winter and spring of 1944, culminating in the disastrous March 30th raid on Nuremberg in which no less than 96 bombers were lost out of an attacking force of 795 aircraft.

When Bomber Command became aware of the Luftwaffe's new homing devices, Monica was removed and air crews were ordered to switch off H2S when not in use. No overall Bomber Command defensive measure was made to counter attacks by the Luftwaffe's new upward firing weapons which allowed the night fighters full rein in their use of *schrage Musik.* Most ventral turrets had been deleted from Mk I/III Lancasters, and from LM522 onwards meant the displacement of under-turrets was necessary in order to accommodate H2S equipment. Improvements in existing defensive turrets were made, and new turrets introduced. An automatic gun-laying apparatus (A.G.L.T.) was fitted to a number of FN20 rear turrets and was pioneered on operations during late 1944 by 49 Squadron. While found to be reasonably effective, war time distribution was limited to several units including 101, 460 and 635 Squadrons. The A.G.L.T. turrets carried .303 guns, whereas the up-dated FN82 turret bore a pair of .50s. From Rose Rice came a new .50 armed turret which was less cluttered internally and whose open-ended canopy offered much better escape for the gunner who, unlike his FN20 colleagues, could carry his parachute inside the turret. No similar improvements were made to nose or upper turrets of Mk I/III aircraft before 1945.

The invasion of Occupied Europe turned Bomber Command from the night raids on German industry to daylight attacks on German Ground forces in France. Lancasters of 5 Group were selectively marked with coloured fins, such aircraft being used as formation leaders of their relative units. 1 Group had a similar facility but concentrated it within 460 Squadron.

Full-scale production of G-H, a precise blind-bombing aid pioneered in late 1943 on Mk IIs, allowed its introduction on 3. Group aircraft during late 1944. G-H allowed for extremely accurate attacks even through 10/10 cloud cover. For daylight raids G-H equipped Lancs sported two parallel yellow bars on the fins and acted as formation/Bombing leaders for non G-H aircraft. No. 3 Group carried out many successful raids during 10/10 cloud conditions both by day and by night, with G-H aircraft providing their own Pathfinder services.

By the last full month of war-time operations (April 1945) the dominance of the Lancaster within Bomber Command reached its peak, no fewer than 56 Squadrons being equipped with the type. Nos. 1, 3 and 5 Groups were fully equipped with Lancs. In addition, No. 8 (PFF) Group which commenced operations in August 1942 with mixed Lancaster/Halifax/Wellington Squadrons, flew only the Lanc as the heavy bomber element within its overall ranks. Apart from the all-Halifax equipped No. 4 Group only the Canadian No. 6 Group operated both heavies, and even here the Lanc equipped 10 of the 17 Squadrons in the Group.

C *Charlie* of 101 Squadron crash landed at her Ludford Magna base on 22 February 1944. The open bay doors suggest they were jammed open. The pipes in the foreground are part of the airfield's FIDO system for fog dispersal. (I.W.M.)

JB172 of 166 Squadron was set on fire by a Bf 110 which was shot down by the badly burned rear gunner. The fire was eventually extinguished but only six men returned — the mid-upper gunner misinterpreted an order from F/O Watson and bailed out to become a POW. (M. Middlebrook)

Armourers hoist 1,000LB bombs into the belly of JO⊙S at Waddington. The fuselage artwork depicts a dog walking away from a tree to which Hitler is clinging and on which the former has discharged his duty. Serialed DV 280 she went missing on the night of 3/4 May 1944. (D. Brett)

Ground crewmen at Skellington prepare ME595 for a sortie during the summer of 1944. The thickened code outline is a result of No. 5 Group's policy of adding yellow outlines to the basic red codes from mid-1944. (M. Gibson)

No. 106 Squadron Lancasters prepare to head out for Frankfurt during March of 1944. The Squadron had flown Manchesters for a short time converting to the Lancaster in early summer 1942.

B. Mk I/III Special (Dambuster)

Bomber Commands only specially formed wartime Squadron was No. 617 Squadron, used to attack the Ruhr Dams on the night of 16/17 May 1943. For this attack Lancaster Mk Is from ED serial block (23 in all) were modified to carry the cylindrical mines intended for use against these specialized targets. Bomb bay doors were removed and the rear of bays were faired in. Pylon mounts were added toward the front of the bay to carry the mines. Belt mechanisms were linked to these mounts to spin the mine before it was released. An original plan to install Ford V8 engines to drive the belt mechanism was abandoned because of their weight, in favor of using the aircraft's undercarriage hydraulic system. Finally all mid-upper turrets were removed and faired over. Three prototypes — ED765/G, 817/G and 825/G — carried out test dropping of the mines; the latter aircraft, ED825/G, however, was not to be one of the 19 aircraft involved in what was to be a successful but costly operation.

On the 16th of May just short of a month after trials were conducted with the new weapon, nineteen Lancasters of No. 617 Squadron lifted off in three waves; one of nine aircraft and two of five. The first wave, of nine, led by Wing Commander Guy Gibson, was to attack the Mohne Dam and if that was breached, go on to attack the Eder Dam. If both targets of the first wave were breached, any aircraft still carrying mines were to assist the attack on the Sorpe which had been detailed to the second wave. The third wave was a mobile reserve under the direct command of No. 5 Group in England.

The Sorpe Dam was damaged, and the Mohne and Eder were breached, flooding the Ruhr Valley drowning some 1200 people and putting much of the Ruhr industry out of action. Of the 19 Lancaster B. Mk III Specials dispatched, eight failed to return.

The surviving G aircraft were remodified back to standard bombers, and reissued, the *Dam Buster* raids were not to be repeated. No. 617 Squadron, between its operational debut and early 1945, was employed in regular pin-point bombing sorties. During this period its Lancasters were mainly standard machines, an exception being the bomb bays which were of the bulged pattern to accommodate the 12,000LB H.C. bomb, and it's aerodynamic off-shoot, the "TallBoy".

Dambusting Bomb Detail

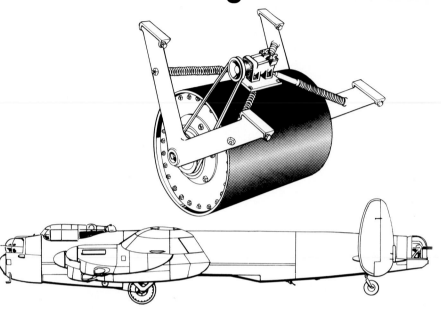

ED825/G carried out test dropping of the cylindrical mines, but was not selected to be one of the attacking aircraft. Underneath can be seen the mine-support pylons and belt drive mechanism for spinning the mine prior to release. The specially fitted .303 can be seen silhouetted just behind the starboard landing gear. (British Official)

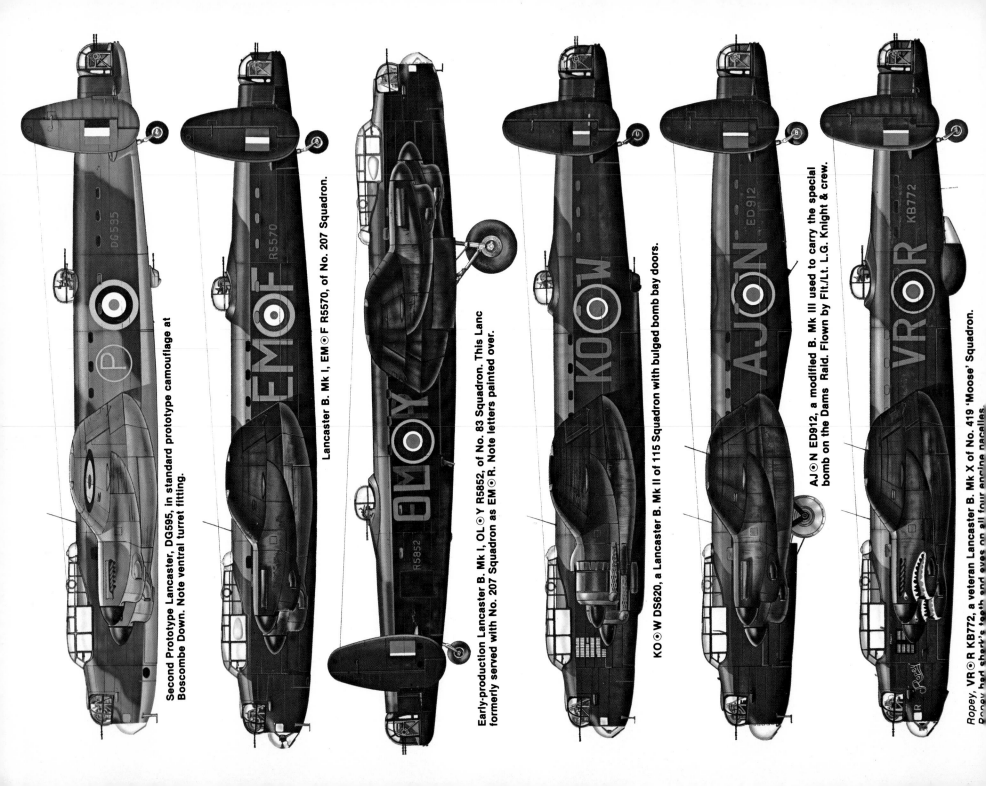

Second Prototype Lancaster, DG595, in standard prototype camouflage at Boscombe Down. Note ventral turret fitting.

Lancaster B. Mk I, EM⊙F R5570, of No. 207 Squadron.

Early-production Lancaster B. Mk I, OL⊙Y R5852, of No. 83 Squadron. This Lanc formerly served with No. 207 Squadron as EM⊙R. Note letters painted over.

KO⊙W DS620, a Lancaster B. Mk II of 115 Squadron with bulged bomb bay doors.

AJ⊙N ED912, a modified B. Mk III used to carry the special bomb on the Dams Raid. Flown by Flt./Lt. L.G. Knight & crew.

Ropey, VR⊙R KB772, a veteran Lancaster B. Mk X of No. 419 'Moose' Squadron. Ropey had shark's teeth and eyes on all four engine nacelles.

Lancaster B. Mk III, DX⊙A LM624, of No. 57 Squadron. Used for daylight raids, the tail markings indicate a flight leaders aircraft.

Lancaster B. Mk I (Special) moments after release of the Grand Slam bomb. YZ⊙J PD119 of No. 617 Squadron in 'day' camouflage scheme. Note the replacement port fin and rudder in 'night' camouflage.

Lancaster B. Mk X

By 1942 Canada's contribution to the Air War effort mainly involved the provision of aircrew training facilities and trained aircrew. Wishing to contribute further an agreement with the Canadian Government was reached resulting in the formation of the Victory Aircraft Company to manufacture Lancasters under license. In August of 1942 R5727 was dispatched to provide a pattern aircraft for the Canadians.

Apart from further alleviating the production load on UK facilities, the presence just across the border of Packard Merlin supplies provided convenient Logistical support. There was a further logistical advantage in fitting engines to available airframes and flying them across the Atlantic as opposed to risking their loss during the protracted and dangerous sea passage.

The first production *Lancaster*, KB700, rolled off the line in September 1943, just thirteen months later. During the ensuing 18 months an additional 430 Lancs were rolled out. Supply of the Mk X was exclusive to No. 6 (Canadian) Group. Initial Mk Xs were powered by Merlin 38s (KB700/774) and Merlin 224s (KB775/999). A similar variation applied to propellers, the original needle-bladed units being superceded by the broader paddle-bladed fittings as of KB774 which provided a superior altitude and rate of climb capabilities.

The provision of the larger bulged bomb doors was felt necessary as was the fitting of ventral turrets. The Mk X's general performance was akin to that of the Mk III, with an all-up weight being slightly reduced to 61,500LBS. Nose, dorsal and rear turrets were initially the standard fittings, but later bombers had their FN50 mid-upper turrets replaced by Martin mid-upper turrets bearing .5 machine guns. The provision of H2S was normally made after delivery of the aircraft to the Group. Wartime supply of the Mk X was almost entirely from the KB production block, delivery being to 419, 420, 425, 428, 431 and 434 Squadrons, although no operational sorties were made by 420 and 425 Squadrons.

The second production block involved 130 aircraft from serial block FM100/299, delivery being made between April and August of 1945 to various Maintenance Units in the U.K. Of this last production block only FM120 made squadron delivery (408 Squadron) before the full-scale return of 6 Group to Canada in May of 1945 for participation in Tiger Force — a plan thwarted by the Japanese surrender in August of 1945.

Dispatched to Canada on 25 August 1942 to be used as the pattern aircraft for Mk X production, R5727 is seen at Prestwick prior to departure. The FN64 ventral turret can be seen very clearly. (British Official)

Returning to Britain during 1944 R5727 has a new framed nose canopy in place of the FN5 turret, a late pattern pitot mast and a faired over navigator's astrodome. Two DF loops are carried, one atop the cockpit canopy and the other below the nose. Canadian civilian registration is CF-CMS. (British Official)

KB700, the first Mk X, on its arrival in Britain. Carrying the name *Ruhr Express* she carries the ventral twin gun mount of the Mk X as well as the bulged bomb bay doors (Canadian Forces)

Ruhr Express was originally assigned to 405 Pathfinder Squadron and later was transferred to No. 6 (Canadian) Group's 419 (Moose) Squadron. The shallow bomb aimers blister carried on arrival has been replaced by a late pattern unit. (Canadian Forces)

(Below) VR⊙X serialed KB732 of 419 Squadron sits broodingly in her Middleton St. George dispersal during the final weeks of the war. An early Mk X she mounts the needle propeller blades and the shallow bomb aimers blister. (Canadian Forces)

The final Mk X to be received was serialed KB999, center aircraft, and was named *Malton Mike*. Assigned to 419 Squadron in March of 1945, she was transferred to 405 Squadron and flew back to Canada. Note the shape of the paddle bladed propellers when compared to the needle propellers below. (Canadian Forces)

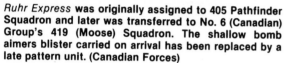

A Defeat

By the Fall of 1943 Bomber Command was unleashing destruction on German cities such as the world had never experienced. Cities like Hamburg, Kassel, Essen, Rostock, Frankfurt, Cologne, the list went on, had nearly ceased to exist. Air Marshal Sir Arthur Harris, Commander-in-Chief of Bomber Command, decided it was time to begin a dampaign of destruction against Berlin, the German capital. On 3 November Harris sent a note to Prime Minister Churchill, "We can wreck Berlin from end to end if the USAAF come in on it. It will cost between us 400-500 aircraft. It will cost Germany the war!" The U.S. Eighth Air Force declined the offer. Harris, however, with Churchill's blessing and acceptance of the fact that a campaign against Berlin was bound to be more costly than an attack on any other major German city, decided to go it alone.

Unfortunately for Bomber Command the Winter of 1943/1944 saw the German night defenses increasing in both strength and effectiveness. The new *Heinkel He 219*, an aircraft specially designed for the night fighter role was now entering service, Ju 88 production had changed over from primarily producing bombers to primarily producing night fighters. *Naxos Z* a device for himing on H2S, and *Flensburg* which picked up and homed on the British tail warning radar Monica were coming into service as well as the new variable frequency *Lichtenstein SN-2 radar*. Just as important as the new equipment was the new tactics of *Frei Nachtjagd* (Free Night Fighting). No longer were the night fighters tied to the tight radar controlled boxes, but the night fighters were at liberty to get into the bomber stream and stay with it until either fuel or ammunition was exhausted, then landings refueling, rearming and go up again. These new tactics and equipment brought on a dramatic increase in RAF losses, losses far in excess of Harris's prediction of 400-500 aircraft. It was not unusual for night fighters to shoot down several bombers on a sortie and for the more experienced German pilots to claim four, five or even six bombers in a single night.

What had been planned as the destruction of Berlin and possibly the end of the war itself, turned into a bitter defeat for Bomber Command. The German capital was hurt but not destroyed. The 400-500 aircraft loss anticipated by Sir Arthur Harris turned out to be over twice as high. During the thirty-five major raids on German targets from 18 November 1943 to 31 March 1944, 1,047 aircraft were lost. It was a brilliant victory for the German defenses — it was their 1ast.

With the invasion of occupied Europe set for June all strategic bomber forces, both British and American, were switched to softening up *Festung Europe*—attacks on German strategic targets virtually ceased.

The new SN2 radar was unaffected by window. Mounted atop the Ju 88 greenhouse can be seen the Naxos 2, its rotating antenna could pick up H2S emissions at a range of 30 miles. (Dr. Briegleb)

(Below Left) The Heinkel He219's increased range, speed and firepower took its toll of Lancasters during the winter of 43/44. Fortunately for Bomber Command there were few of them. (Helmut Rosenboom)

Mounted midway down the spine of this Ju 88G can be seen the oblique upward firing schrage Musik that took a terrible toll of Lancasters during the Berlin Campaign. (G. Stafford)

An early production machine, WS⊙S/W4380 of 9 Squadron is seen visiting the B-17 base at Glatton (457th BG). This machine also served with 50 and 12 Squadron and later had her serial number changed to 4886M. (M. Gibson)

Bomb Aimers Bubble

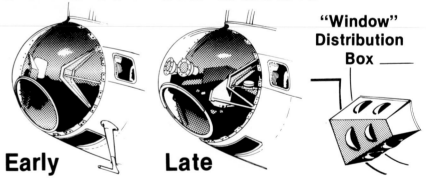

"Window" Distribution Box

Early **Late**

(Above Left) LM583 of 467 Squadron carrying a White tail with a dark cross is a daylight formation leader. After D-Day, Bomber Command began carrying out regular daylight operations but retained the night camouflage scheme. Coming on strength in May LM583 was lost in the 29/30 July night raid on Königsberg. (British Official)

"C"onquering "C"leo of 630 Squadron based at East Kirkby vents her anger upon the Nazi Flag. On transfer to 617 Squadron P/O Watts, leaning out the window, 'borrowed' this bomber, flying several operations in her before No. 630 firmly requested Cleo's return. (G. Copeman)

Black-Red formation leader fin marking variation is carried on LE⊙F/LM259. The aircraft carries 15 bomb symbols and the name *Spirit of Canada* will be added shortly. (G. Copeman)

Lose one, gain one. DX⊙A/LM624 replaced DX⊙A/ND471 after the latter was successfully ditched by P/O Nicklin on 21/22 June 1944. The same crew then took over the new A Able. She carries the Black-Red fin markings of a No. 5 Group formation leader and the yellow edged codes, also a 5 Group feature. (G. Copeman)

Three Lancasters of 75 (New Zealand) Squadron taxi out for a daylight Op during mid-1944. Two have the bulged bomb bay doors, but the furthest aircraft is not equipped with H2S. (C. Bishop)

Pathfinder units were prime enemy targets. LQ⊙K/ME315 of 405 Squadron, the only Canadian Pathfinder Squadron. The bomber not only survived this extreme damage but also the war. (H. Holmes)

With flaps at 30 degrees and radiator shutters open, a fellow 15 Squadron bomber awaits the take-off of LS⊙N/PA170 for a daylight raid on Essen. N Nan crashed landed in Holland on 1 January 1945. (D. Clarke)

One for luck! Flt/Lt. Constable pats the art work on TC⊙A/ND992, a No. 170 Squadron machine. The bomber survived the war but, sadly Constable was K.I.A. over Neuss on the night of 21/22 February 1945. (A. Simpson)

Olivia, a 170 Squadron mate of TC⊙A bears the needle-bladed propellers, late pattern pitot mast and the Yellow gas patch circle borne by No. 1 Group Lancasters. (A. Simpson)

Now preserved in the Museum at RAF Hendon PO⊙S/R5868 or *S For Sugar* as it became known, is probably the most famous of Lancasters. Seen here in 1944 with 98 bomb symbols, she has the original pattern pitot mast and bomb aimers blister as well as the needle-bladed propellers. The windscreen glycol sprays (windshield washers) can be seen mounted in front of the cockpit. (I.W.M.)

S For Sugar at Sudbury (486th BG) in early 1945. *Sugar* has undergone a face lift which includes a late pattern pitot mast and bomb aimers blister, paddle blade propellers and the addition of the Rebbeca H shaped aerials. The cockpit observation blister has also disappeared. Bomb silhouettes now tally 125. (I.W.M.)

Needle Bladed Propellers

Paddle Bladed Propellers

Rebecca

Early Pitot Mast

Late Pitot Mast

Cockpit Observation Blister

Windscreen Washer

QB⊙P/NG347 *Picadilly Princess*, heavily laden with bombs, pulls into the bright morning sky. The nubile young lady adorning the nose was seen on the aircraft of several airforces, each with their own title. (Canadian Forces Photo)

Sky Floosie of No. 44 (Rhodesia) Squadron alongside a presentation fuel Bowser. Aircraft tail in center background displays the unit's daylight formation leader markings, a Black cross on a Red background. (British Official)

Cockpit view of Flight Officer Young's PM⊙D/JB555. On the right center console the top four dials show engine boost while the bottom four records engine revolutions. (L. Young)

A4⊙E of 115 Squadron's 'C' Flight is waved off on an operation during 1944 carrying unusual letter/number codes. Several Bomber Command units had a similar separation in code markings between the main squadron compliment and the relative C flight. (A.T. Douglas)

Cockpit view within EM⊙M/ED802 as the pilot Sgt. J. Mackintosh and Flight Engineer Sgt. R. Sooley scrutinize the latter's main panel prior to start up. Pilot's head armor is clearly depicted in upper left corner of photo. (J. Mackintosh)

Sgt. Hyde of Mackintosh's crew at the Wireless position tuning his TR1154/55 radio equipment. Crew belonged to No. 207 Squadron then based at Langer. (J. Mackintosh)

(Above) Summer of 1944 sees LS⊙C/ME844 of No. 15 Squadron carrying standard red codes located in normal port side position as well as twenty bomb symbols painted under the pilot's position. (D. Clarke)

(Above Left) Propeller change on No. 431 (Iroquois) Squadron's SE⊙L is affected with the aid of a mobile crane. (Canadian Forces Photo)

(Below Left) Crew photo from 44 Squadron shows off the variations of flight gear found on most aircrew. Of special note is the variety of foot wear including shoes with separate leggings and full length fur boots - the only suitable footwear for gunners. (I.W.M.)

(Below) An echelon of Lancasters belonging to No. 300 Squadron, Bomber Command's only Polish heavy bomber unit. (D. Clarke)

This 100 op' veteran carries the world in a ring trailing stars like a comet adorning the nose, coded UL⊙I and serialed LM227 this machine forms a backdrop for both air and ground crew to have their picture taken at Fiskerton during April 1945. (D. Clarke)

Another 100 op' veteran, A Able's air and ground crew pose somewhat less sedately than those of the previous photo. (D. Clarke)

A late winter ice storm at Mildenhall provides a spectacular scene for a machine from 149 Squadron. Fin markings of two parallel bars indicate that the machine was a G-H daylight formation leader. (K. Batchelor)

Champagne Charlie **NN757** of No. 625 Squadron at war's end wears unshrouded exhausts. To increase efficiency the exhaust shrouds were dispensed with as quickly as possible. (C. Koder)

Lancasters were put into immediate service ferrying troops home, first those POWs who were fit to travel and then regular Army. (C. Koder)

Shorn of her armament and ABC aerials Z Zebra of No. 101 Squadron thunders down the Pomegliano runway while engaged in evacuating troops from Italy to Britain. (C. Koder)

NN616/ZN⊙J of No. 106 Squadron lies broken beside Metheringham's FIDO pipes after crash landing. Her back is broken just behind the mid-upper turret, but she was subsequently restored to service. (D. Clarke)

74,000 exPOWs were ferried back to Britain safely, however RF230, loaded with 25 passengers tragically crashed after take off killing all on board. (D. Clarke)

39

ME844 now sports new White script pattern Squadron codes and a new individual aircraft letter. Bomb log tally is 78. Clover leaf shape just ahead of the mid-upper turret is a gas detection patch. (C. Clarke)

Lancaster B. Mk I (Special)

The introduction of the Lancaster B. Mk I (Special) in early 1945 was a direct result of the concurrent advent of the ultimate in conventional bombing weapon — the 22,000LB *Grand Slam*, the largest bomb carried by an aircraft during WWII. Such aircraft were literally gutted out to carry the huge load. Bomb bay doors were removed and the bomb bay was faired in at both ends, Merlin 24 engines were fitted and the undercarriage was strengthened. PB529/G and PB995/G made ground and air tests during February 1945 and although the latter initially flew with all turrets in position most Mk I Specials had the nose and mid-upper turrets removed and to reduce weight even further the rear turrets were reduced to a single pair of .303s. At 73,000LBS loaded, these *Lancasters* had an approximate range of 1,650 miles on a reduced fuel capacity of 1,675 gallons; flying from airfield on the continent such range was sufficient to reach specialist targets when *Grand Slam* made its debut in March 1945. Even the well-tried Lancaster, however, was hard pressed to lift *Grand Slam* much beyond 17,000FT which was somewhat lower than its designer, Barnes Wallis, felt was the most effective height for maximum penetration. Practical results were to bely such doubts, and 41 bombs were used to full effect before the war's end, usually obliterating their targets or so heavily damaging them as to make further use by the enemy fruitless.

Between 1945 and 1946 No. 15 Squadron took over some *Specials* with which the unit's crews conducted bombing trials in concert with USAAF B-29s modified to carry *Grand Slam*, on several U-Boat pens. The bombs were filled with solid weights in order to test the bomb's penetration power. By 1948 the Mk I Specials had been largely scrapped.

Ballistic companion and forerunner to Grand Slam was the 12,000LB Tall Boy. This Tall Boy affords comparison with a 4LB practice bomb being held by the airman. (I.W.M.)

A B. Mk I (Special) with its Grand Slam about to be hoisted into the bomb bay. Scheme is the temperate scheme with upper fin markings in White, YZ codes were borne by Grand Slam aircraft. (Canadian Forces Photo)

PD995 photographed during flight tests of Grand Slam, whose great 22,000LB mass can be seen hanging from its concave belly. In common with other specials, PD995 had the nose and dorsal turrets removed and faired over. Rear turrets were mainly fitted with a pair of .5 machine guns. (D. Clarke)

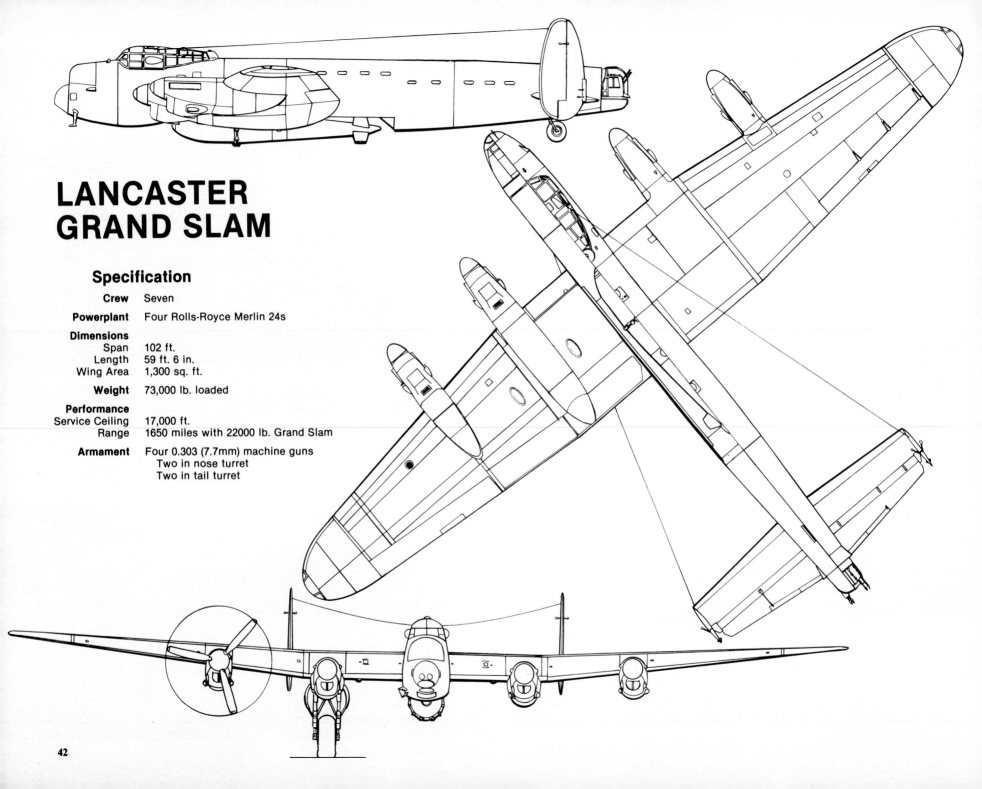

LANCASTER
GRAND SLAM

Specification

Crew   Seven

Powerplant   Four Rolls-Royce Merlin 24s

Dimensions
Span   102 ft.
Length   59 ft. 6 in.
Wing Area   1,300 sq. ft.

Weight   73,000 lb. loaded

Performance
Service Ceiling   17,000 ft.
Range   1650 miles with 22000 lb. Grand Slam

Armament   Four 0.303 (7.7mm) machine guns
    Two in nose turret
    Two in tail turret

Lancaster B. Mk I(FE)

By 1944 attention was being turned to providing a heavy bomber force to supplement the USAAF assault on Japan. Anxious to take her place alongside American Forces in defeating Japan, a team was sent to the States to investigate the possibility of using the new B-29 Superfortress. It was decided, however, to use the new Lincoln, with the Lancaster as an interim bomber. In order to increase the range of the Lancaster, experiments were conducted with two (HK541 and SW244) B. Mk Is being modified to have saddle tanks of 1200 gallons capacity installed on the spine of the aircraft just behind the cockpit. Flight characteristics caused the abandonment of the program.

The initial intention was to equip *Tiger Force* (as the Far East Command had become known) with Lincolns but the production line disruption and consequent delay caused the plans abandonment. Instead, B. Mk I Lancasters from Metropolitan Vicker's RA serial block and Armstrong-Whitworth's SW series were selected for modification to Far East Operational requirements. Such bombers were first delivered to No. 38 Maintenance Unit and from there sent to Harland and Wolfe in Belfast, Ireland for adaptation. The need to operate over the large stretch of water between the Marianas and Japan was recognized by the installation of several precise navigation and homing aides such as Loran, H2S Mk II, GH, and Rebecca II.

In-flight refueling was investigated and orders were even issued to prepare 600 Lancasters as tankers for 600 Lincolns before plans were changed. As an alternative, 400 gallons of fuel were to be carried in the bomb bay at the expense of the FN50 mid-upper turret. Nose and tail turrets on the Mk I(FE) were the FN5 and FN82 respectively, the latter, bearing a pair of 0.5 machine guns. European camouflage schemes being considered largely unnecessary for the Far East, all top and side surfaces were sprayed white and anti-searchlight black was applied underneath.

SW244 in Australia in November 1945. The cockpit area was cut down and faired into the saddle tank shape. Exhaust shrouds are carried as is the standard European color scheme. Both bombers were scrapped in November 1946. (G. Cunningham)

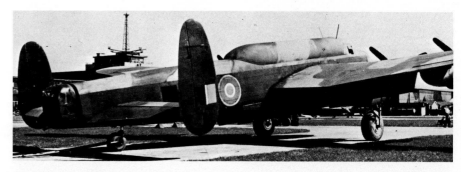

One of the two Mk I Lancasters fitted with 1200 gallon capacity saddle tanks, which supplemented the normal 2154 gallons carried in six wing tanks. Flown to India for trials that were less than successful. (British Official)

Long-range Saddle Tanks

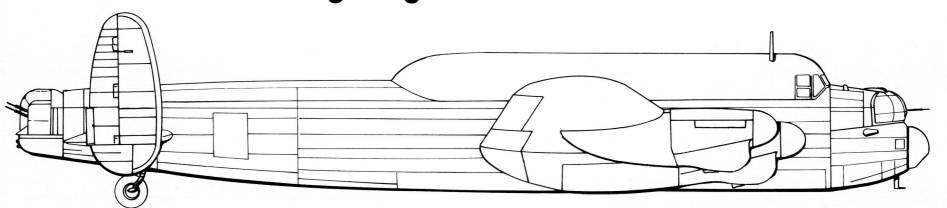

Echelon formation of No. 35 Squadron B. Mk I(FE)s during their tour of the USA illustrates the variation in bulged and standard bomb bay doors fitted, and the absence of under wing roundels. (RAF Museum)

Looking back from the astrodome of a 115 Squadron Lancaster B. Mk I(FE) clearly depicts the offset arrangement of the upper fuselage aerials borne by the majority of Lancasters. (G. Russell)

(Top Left) TW657 carries the revised serial number layout carried on some Mk I(FE) bombers. The codes are believed to be in black. The addition of a pair of 0.5 machine guns made for a much more spacious FN82 turret. (J.C. Scutts)

KO⊙B/PA415 of No. 115 Squadron sharing the airfield with Mosquitoes. Bomb doors appear to be standard pattern. Sides of the engine cowlings have been darkened to hide engine exhaust. (G. Russell)

Lancaster B. Mk VII(FE)

Prototype for the Lancaster Mk VII(FE) variant was NN801, built by Austin (Longbridge), and the forerunner of 230 aircraft in the NX series to be turned out by the company and originally scheduled for Tiger Force. The main external change was to have been the replacement of the FN50 mid-upper turret by an American-produced Martin frameless unit, and relocated to a point just behind the wing trailing edge. In contrast to the FN turret it was electrically operated.

The term *Interim* referred unofficially to airframes NX548/589 and NX603/610. Delays in the supply of the Martin turrets resulted in these aircraft being issued as standard Mk I bombers — apart from the setting of the FN50 turrets in the intended location for the Martin turrets. With the exception of NX558, which went to Avro, all saw service prior to VE Day. Re-positioning the mid-upper turret above the bomb bay created problems in fore and aft crew movement, but afforded the mid-upper gunner easier access and, more importantly, much greater escape facility compared to the normal turret location.

The Martin turret was available for inclusion in the main production block, NX611/794, FN82 rear turrets also being fitted, both units bearing a pair of .5 Browning Mk II machine guns. Although all up weight on these aircraft was set at 72,000LBS, the Mark VII(FE) had a general performance akin to that of the Mk I. In contrast to the *Interim* batch whose delivery was in many cases made to No. 32 and 38 Maintenance Units, Mk VII(FE) equipped Squadrons included Nos. 9, 12, 40, 70, 104 and 617.

In contrast to the Mk I(FE) equipped units, the Mk VII(FE) Squadrons were mainly employed overseas.

Believed to be in the Middle East sometime between 1946 and 1947, NX727 of No. 38 Squadron displays the Black/White scheme borne by the Mk VII(FE). The more streamlined Martin mid-upper turret just behind the wing trailing edge, bulged bomb bay doors and a clear H2S radome, were all regular features of the Mk VII(FE) variant. Codes and serial are in Red. (B. Robertson)

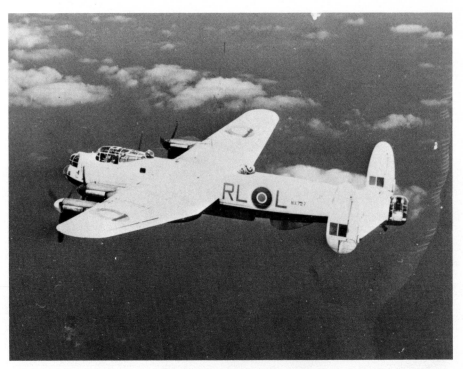

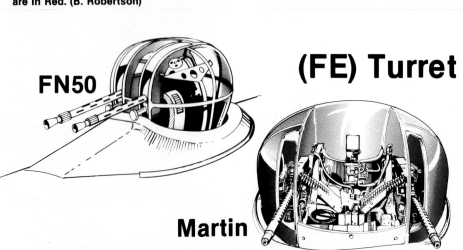

FN50

(FE) Turret

Martin

Wing Commander Calder's crew in front of NX687 prior to the Commander-in-Chief's tour of South America during 1945. The latter's presence on the trip is indicated by his personal rank pennant flying ahead of the cockpit and also painted below the cockpit. (K. Batchelor)

No. 617 Squadron displays its Mk VII(FE) Lancasters to a large crowd at Salbani, India during 1946, with a low level pass. (J. Flynn)

H2S Radome

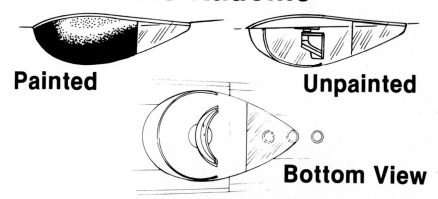

Painted

Unpainted

Bottom View

(Top Left) NX758 of No. 9 Squadron stands in its dispersal at Salbani, her engine cowlings showing heavy exhaust smoke stains. The Squadron accompanied 617 Squadron to India in 1946, both returning to Britain before the year's end. (L. Moore)

KC⊙G/NX783 of No. 617 Squadron is equipped with standard bomb bay doors in contrast to the general Mk VII(FE) configuration. The Squadron badge is prominently displayed on the nose. (J. Flynn)

One of 54 bombers [32 Mk I (FE)s and 22 Mk VII(FE)s] supplied to the French Navy around 1948, this Mk VII variant has an added rear section to the exhaust shrouds and the replacement of the Martin turret with an escape hatch. Color scheme is overall Gloss Royal Blue. (H. Holmes)

This French Navy Mk VII carries an all White color scheme adopted subsequent to going into service. Note the Black area on the cowls in order to conceal the exhaust stains. (B. Robertson)

Resplendent in a Dark Gray/Black color pattern, NX739 is serving with Eagle Aviation on photographic duties. All turrets have been retained as have the bulged bomb bay doors. (B. Robertson)

A.S.R./G.R./M.R. III Lancaster

The general dependence of the RAF on American Air Sea Rescue equipment left an immediate post-war gap when US aircraft were disposed of under the terms of Lend Lease. The gap was hastily filled in late 1945 by converting a number of Lancaster Mk IIIs from the serial blocks of RE, RF and SW. The firm of Cunliffe Owen carried out the task of fitting external attachments upon which life boats could be suspended under the aircraft. Initial supplies of the Air Sea Rescue III Lancaster (A.S.R. III Lancaster) were made to No. 279 Squadron at Thornaby; a separate Flight, No. 1348, was subsequently formed from the Squadron and dispatched in late 1945 to Burma. In late 1946 the Flight returned to the Middle East where it was disbanded, its Lancasters being incorporated into the ranks of No. 37 and 38 Squadrons. During 1948 these units in turn moved to Malta where they operated a full complement of A.S.R. IIIs and Mk VII(FE). The same codes (RL) were used by all three units, but upon No. 37 Squadron's return to the UK in 1951, No. 38 reverted to displaying only individual aircraft letters.

The first full Squadron based in the UK was No. 179, which had been formed from No. 279 Squadron in 1946, and then split in 179X and 179Y Squadrons; 179Y later became No. 210 Squadron. At about the same time three more Squadrons were established on the A.S.R. III, 120, 203 and 224, with 224 being disbanded in December of 1946.

By 1947 the need for an interim General Reconnaissance (GR) aircraft had forced the conversion of Air Sea Rescue Lancasters to General Reconnaissance, with the installation of ASV Radar. A further change of title (and relative function) to Maritime Reconnaissance (MR) occurred around 1950. By this time the later Lincoln style undercarriage was being found in these aircraft. In addition to operational units, No. 236 Operational Training Unit (OTU) at Kinloss and the School of Maritime Reconnaissance at St. Mawgan made use of G.R. Lancasters, receiving it's aircraft after the front line Squadrons had dispensed with their services.

The aircrafts' external outline was little changed during their lifetime. The mid-upper turret was removed and faired over and windows were added just ahead of the tailplane for observation purposes. In addition, a rearward-facing camera in an extended pod was mounted under the rear turret on G.R. and M.R. aircraft. H2S was a standard fitting.

Initial color schemes on these aircraft was a temperate Green/Gray on top with Light Gray undersurfaces. About 1950 a change was made to White undersurfaces and Gray top surfaces. Variations in fuselage demarcation lines was found, some with the White extending onto the top of the wing leading edge. An overall Gray-blue was carried by a number of M.R. IIIs.

(Above and Below) RL⊙A/RF310 carrying her lifeboat in late 1945. A few months later she is a sad wreck at Pegu in Burma where she was serving with 1348 Flt. (B. Robertson)

A.S.R. Mk III with Lifeboat

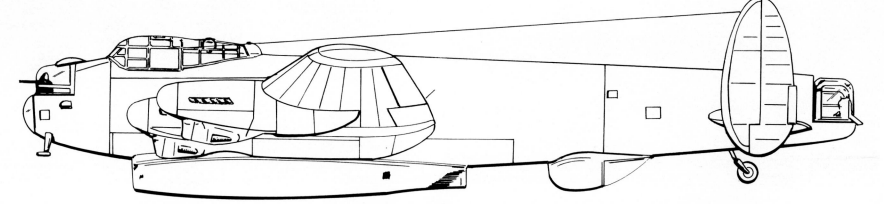

PA475 was a Mk III modified to photographic reconnaissance standards. Bomber is seen at Eastleigh in Kenya as part of 82 Squadron's C Flight which made extensive mapping surveys of Central Africa between 1946 and 1952. Note the fairing behind the cockpit and the fairing over the nose turret position. (B. Robertson)

(Above) Bearing the ultimate coastal command color scheme of overall Grey Blue, SW366 was an ASR/GRIII which saw varied service with the school of Maritime Reconnaissance during the early 1950s. (B. Robertson)

Although actually a Lancastrian C.II, VM703 typifies the general use of the Lancaster design as an engine test bed. In this case, two DeHavilland Ghost jets supplant the outer Merlins. In addition, two booster units under the rear fuselage provide further take-off thrust. (H. Holmes)